W9-BPL-260

FEB 2019

Germany

SEAN CORBETT

MEDIA ENHANCED BOOKS
AV2 BY WEIGL
ADDED VALUE · AUDIO VISUAL

3 1150 01652 9352

BOISE PUBLIC LIBRARY

www.av2books.com

AV² provides enriched content that supplements and complements this book. Weigl's AV² books strive to create inspired learning and engage young minds in a total learning experience.

Your AV² Media Enhanced books come alive with...

Audio
Listen to sections of the book read aloud.

Key Words
Study vocabulary, and complete a matching word activity.

Video
Watch informative video clips.

Quizzes
Test your knowledge.

Embedded Weblinks
Gain additional information for research.

Slide Show
View images and captions, and prepare a presentation.

Go to www.av2books.com, and enter this book's unique code.

BOOK CODE

E 6 9 5 6 7 4

AV² by Weigl brings you media enhanced books that support active learning.

Try This!
Complete activities and hands-on experiments.

... and much, much more!

Published by AV² by Weigl
350 5th Avenue, 59th Floor
New York, NY 10118
Website: www.av2books.com

Copyright © 2017 AV² by Weigl
All rights reserved. No part of this publication may be reproduced, stored in a retrieval system, or transmitted in any form or by any means, electronic, mechanical, photocopying, recording, or otherwise, without the prior written permission of the publisher.

Library of Congress Cataloging-in-Publication Data

Names: Corbett, Sean, author.
Title: Germany / Sean Corbett.
Description: New York, NY : AV2 by Weigl, 2016. | Series: Exploring countries | Includes index.
Identifiers: LCCN 2015049788 (print) | LCCN 2015049872 (ebook) | ISBN 9781489646071 (hard cover : alk. paper) | ISBN 9781489650252 (soft cover : alk. paper) | ISBN 9781489646088 (Multi-User eBook)
Subjects: LCSH: Germany--Juvenile literature. | Germany--Description and travel--Juvenile literature.
Classification: LCC DD17 .C67 2016 (print) | LCC DD17 (ebook) | DDC 943--dc23
LC record available at http://lccn.loc.gov/2015049788

Printed in the United States of America in Brainerd, Minnesota
1 2 3 4 5 6 7 8 9   20 19 18 17 16

032016
150316

Project Coordinator Heather Kissock
Art Director Terry Paulhus

Photo Credits
Every reasonable effort has been made to trace ownership and to obtain permission to reprint copyright material. The publishers would be pleased to have any errors or omissions brought to their attention so that they may be corrected in subsequent printings.

Weigl acknowledges Corbis Images and Getty Images as its primary photo suppliers for this title.

2 Exploring Countries

Contents

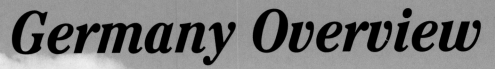

Germany Overview

Germany is one of the largest and most populated countries on the continent of Europe. It has tall mountain peaks, dense forests, and large cities. For many years, Germany had great military power. It was split into two countries, West and East Germany, after it lost World War II in 1945. Reunited in 1990, Germany is now one of the richest countries in the world. It has the fifth-largest **economy** of any nation, and the country is a major steel and automobile producer. Germany is known for its high-speed national highway system called the *autobahn*.

In 1961, the East German government built the Berlin Wall around the city of West Berlin to keep citizens from entering West Germany. It remained a barrier until 1989. Parts of the wall are now a memorial.

Frankfurt is one of Germany's oldest cities. Its opera house is the site of jazz, rock, and classical concerts.

Germany is known for its knotted salted bread, called *brezel*.

Millions of people come to the city of Munich each year for the autumn festival called Oktoberfest.

Several castles on the Rhine River date back centuries, including Marksburg Castle.

Exploring *Germany*

Germany covers 137,847 square miles (357,022 square kilometers). To the north are Denmark, the Baltic Sea, and the North Sea. Germany borders Poland and the Czech Republic to the east. The Netherlands, Belgium, Luxembourg, and France are to the west. Austria and Switzerland are to the south. Germany's tallest mountains are in the southeast. On the country's northern coast, the **altitude** drops to just below sea level.

North Sea

United Kingdom

Belgium

Black Forest

France

Map Legend

Germany	Rhine River	Capital City
Land	Zugspitze	SCALE
Water	Black Forest	

250 Miles

250 Kilometers

Black Forest

The Black Forest is located in southwestern Germany. It covers an area of 2,320 square miles (6,009 sq. km). The Black Forest was named after its many dark-colored fir trees.

Denmark

Baltic Sea

Poland

Netherlands

Rhine River

Berlin

Berlin

GERMANY

Luxembourg

Czech Republic

Zugspitze

Switzerland

Austria

Rhine River

The Rhine is Germany's longest river. It starts in Switzerland and flows north into Germany, where it forms part of the German–French border. The Rhine continues through northern Germany to the Netherlands.

Zugspitze

The Zugspitze is the highest peak in Germany. Located on the border with Austria, it stands 9,718 feet (2,962 meters) tall. The peak offers beautiful views.

Berlin

Berlin is the capital and largest city in Germany. It was founded in the early 13th century. Today, 3.5 million people live in Berlin.

LAND AND CLIMATE

Germany contains a wide variety of landscapes. In central Germany, there is a mixture of forested mountains, **plateaus**, and **basins**. This natural region is called the Central Uplands. An area of low flat land called the North German Plain extends across northern Germany. Most of the land is barely above sea level.

Several mountain ranges cover parts of Germany. In the south is the country's largest mountain range, the Bavarian Alps. The Rhön mountains in central Germany were created by ancient volcanoes. In the southwestern part of the country, rounded hills and mountains run along the Rhine River valley. They are called the Eifel and the Hunsrück ranges. In the east, the Ore Mountains form part of the Czech border.

The Fichtelberg cable car, the oldest in Germany, carries passengers almost 1,000 feet (300 m) up a mountainside in the Ore Mountains.

Most rivers in Germany flow north and then into the North Sea. One exception is the Danube. It runs east from the Black Forest through Germany and several other countries before it empties into the Black Sea.

Germany's major rivers also include the Elbe and the Oder. The Elbe runs from the Czech Republic into eastern Germany and then north. The Oder forms part of the border between Poland and Germany. The Moselle River starts in France, passes through Luxembourg, and flows into the Rhine in Germany.

The climate in Germany varies from region to region. The north has warm summers, along with high levels of humidity and long stretches of rainfall. Moist air is brought to the region by winds blowing in from the North Sea. Temperatures in the south have greater extremes. Southeastern Germany has the coldest winters in the country. The hottest summers occur in the southwest.

Land and Climate BY THE NUMBERS

1,484 Miles
Length of the coastline of Germany. (2,388 km)

765 Miles
Total length of the Rhine River. (1,230 km)

209 Square Miles
Area of Lake Constance in southern Germany, the country's largest lake. (541 sq. km)

The Moselle River measures about 340 miles (545 km) long. Near the German city of Koblenz, the river's banks are home to many of Germany's vineyards.

PLANTS AND ANIMALS

Germany has large forests of oak, beech, and birch trees. Some of the native trees were cut down. Since then, newly planted pine and spruce have helped restore the forests. Hepatica and several other kinds of wildflowers grow in the **alpine** regions in the south. In the north, sea lavender grows along the coast. Chamomile, edelweiss, and cornflower are native to the country.

Deer and foxes are common in the forests of Germany. Lynx also roam there. Birds that live in the country year-round include sparrows, owls, woodpeckers, herons, and falcons. Quail, pheasant, and ibex live in the Alps.

Gray horned heath sheep are native to Germany and other areas of northern Europe. As the region was developed for farms and settlements, the sheep lost grassy land to feed on. Herds of these sheep now live in a protected area in northern Germany.

Plants and Animals by the NUMBERS

32% Portion of Germany that is covered by forests.

175 Pounds Weight of the heaviest male gray horned heath sheep. (80 kilograms)

71 Number of tree **species** in Germany.

15 Number of national parks in Germany.

Germany is home to more than 2 million wild boars.

NATURAL RESOURCES

Germany is a major producer of coal. The Ruhr River valley in the western part of the country has one of the world's largest **coalfields**. Coal is also found to the east, in the Lower Lusatia region. Bituminous coal, a type of black coal that produces a great deal of heat when burned, is one of Germany's main energy sources. It is second only to oil, which comes mostly from other countries. Germany also mines lignite, a brown coal of lesser quality.

Salt and **potash** are mined near the Harz mountains in northern Germany. Trees are another major resource. German forests are a source of valuable timber.

Some of Germany's richest soil is in the northern part of the Central Uplands. The Rhine valley near the Alps also has rich soil. Land with good soil is valuable for growing crops and for animal grazing. Germany's main crops include wheat, barley, corn, sugar beets, and potatoes.

Natural Resources BY THE NUMBERS

48% Portion of the land in Germany used for growing crops and raising livestock.

1ST Germany's rank among the world's lignite producers.

45% Portion of German electricity generated from burning coal.

Much of the coal mined in Germany is used in power plants that produce electricity.

TOURISM

Germany is a destination for tourists from around the world. Visitors who enjoy nature go to the Rhine River valley and the Black Forest. People interested in history can view castles, old churches, and museums. Villages built many centuries ago are not far from the skyscrapers of Germany's modern cities.

Berlin is the country's main **urban** center. The city is home to more than 400 art galleries, the Berlin Opera, and the annual Berlin Film Festival. Many tourists also visit the Allied Museum, which has exhibits on recent German history.

The city of Potsdam, near Berlin, has many interesting sights. Park Sanssouci includes a palace that was a summer home for King Frederick II. The city's large landscaped parks became a **UNESCO** World Heritage site in 1990.

Checkpoint Charlie was a crossing point between East and West Berlin after World War II. Today, tourists visit a reconstruction of the guardhouse at the Allied Museum.

Sanssouci Palace was completed in 1747. The building, which features a large central dome, overlooks many gardens.

Munich, near the Bavarian Alps, is sometimes called "Germany's secret capital." Many museums and shopping areas make it popular with tourists. The Deutsches Museum in Munich is one of the world's oldest museums of technology and engineering. It attracts more than 1.4 million visitors each year.

Not far from Munich is Neuschwanstein Castle. This elaborate building rests on a rock ledge in the Bavarian Alps. Construction began in 1869, under orders from Bavaria's King Louis II. Also nearby, on the Danube River in the southern city of Ulm, is one of the tallest church buildings in the world. The tower of Ulm Münster reaches 530 feet (162 m).

Tourists in western Germany visit Cologne. This city is home to the largest **Gothic** cathedral in northern Europe. It took more than 600 years to build Cologne Cathedral, or Kölner Dom. People also visit Museum Ludwig to see its large collection of modern art.

Tourism
BY THE NUMBERS

1903 Year the Deutsches Museum was founded.

768 Number of steps in the tower of the Ulm Münster.

700 ACRES Area of Park Sanssouci. (300 hectares)

40 Number of UNESCO World Heritage sites in Germany, including Cologne Cathedral.

Neuschwanstein Castle is one of Germany's most popular attractions. It inspired the Sleeping Beauty Castle at the California theme park Disneyland.

INDUSTRY

Germany is one of the world's top-10 steel-producing nations. Much of the country's steel is used by the automobile industry. Germany produces more automobiles than any other country except Japan, the United States, and China. About three-fourths of the cars produced in Germany are **exported**.

Germany has Europe's largest industry manufacturing chemicals and chemical products. Items made by this industry include cleaning products, cosmetics, and paints. Most factories are located along the Rhine River.

Manufacturing appliances and technology products is also a major industry in Germany. Osram, Siemens, and AEG produce items including ovens, mobile phones, and light bulbs. Their factories are mainly located in southern Germany.

BMW, Mercedes-Benz, Audi, Volkswagen, and Porsche are the best-known German car brands.

Industry BY THE NUMBERS

25% Portion of German workers with jobs in industry.

More Than **750,000** Number of workers in the automobile industry.

1.7 MILLION Number of Mercedes-Benz cars sold in 2014.

GOODS AND SERVICES

Most German workers are employed in service industries. These workers provide services instead of producing goods. Some of the largest service industries in Germany are **retailing**, banking, and insurance. Service workers also include teachers, doctors, nurses, bus drivers, and hotel clerks.

Although Germany sells goods to countries all over the world, most of its trade is with other members of the **European Union** (EU). Germany also sells many goods to the United States. Major exports include chemical and electronics products, as well as food and wine.

Many of Germany's **imports** come from other EU countries and from China. Raw materials are brought in for German industries. Hamburg is Germany's main port. Goods are transported to the interior of the country by water, rail, and road. The German road system is the third-largest in the world.

Goods and Services BY THE NUMBERS

74% Portion of German workers with jobs in service industries.

6% Percentage of imports that come from China.

427 Number of merchant marine vessels, or ships that carry goods, in Germany.

27,000 Miles Total length of railways in Germany. (43,000 km)

About one-third of Germany's imports enter the country through the port of Hamburg.

INDIGENOUS PEOPLES

E vidence found in caves in southwestern Germany suggests that **prehistoric** peoples lived there tens of thousands of years in the past. About 40,000 to 28,000 years ago, the Aurignacian culture was one of the first groups to produce art that showed people. In southern Germany, scientists have found a prehistoric settlement called Pestenacker that is more than 5,500 years old.

By about 600 BC, Celtic people were living in southern Germany. Germanic tribes began to move down from the Baltic Sea region around 500 BC. They fought and joined with the Celts. About 400 years later, along the Rhine and Danube Rivers, they clashed with armies of the Roman **Empire**.

By the first century AD, a small part of western Germany was a **Roman province**. However, Germanic tribes fought off several attempts by Roman armies to conquer their lands. In the following centuries, Germanic tribes took over parts of the Roman Empire for themselves.

Indigenous Peoples BY THE NUMBERS

ABOUT 35,000 YEARS OLD
Age of a carving made from mammoth ivory found in a cave near Stetten.

17 Number of prehistoric houses found in the Pestenacker settlement.

58 BC

Year that Germanic tribes started fighting the army of Roman leader Julius Caesar.

Many bridges built by the Romans in Germany are still in use today.

EARLY KINGDOMS

In AD 476, a German leader named Odovacar and his troops entered the city of Rome and removed the last Roman emperor. Odovacar set up a kingdom in Italy. At this time, many Germanic tribes were spread across Germany and Italy. Some of the largest tribes were the Goths, Alemanni, Saxons, and Franks.

The Franks came to rule the land between the Rhine and Elbe Rivers, and they also conquered other regions of Europe. In 800, Charlemagne, king of the Franks, became emperor of this large area. It was called the Holy Roman Empire.

In the ninth century, an agreement called the Treaty of Verdun split the Frankish empire. Starting in 919, most of Germany was ruled by the Liudolf, or Saxon, **dynasty**. Otto I, who became the Saxon king in 936, conquered lands in other parts of Europe. He was later crowned Holy Roman emperor.

At Least 18 Number of children that Charlemagne had during his life.

843 Year the Treaty of Verdun was signed.

962 Year Otto I became Holy Roman emperor.

Pope Leo III crowned Charlemagne emperor at a ceremony in Rome, Italy.

THE AGE OF EXPANSION

After Otto I, various German rulers held and lost power. In the 1200s, Friedrich II was a strong German king and Holy Roman emperor. Following Friedrich's death, German kings became less powerful. Princes or other rulers of small German states acted with more independence.

In 1517, religious leader Martin Luther started the Protestant Reformation. This was a protest against many practices of the Roman Catholic Church. At the time, almost all Germans were Roman Catholics. Many German princes supported Luther. Over time, northern Germany became largely Protestant. Southern Germany remained mainly Catholic. Wars over religion involving German states lasted for more than a century. One of those wars began in 1618 and went on for 30 years.

Martin Luther wrote a list of 95 theses, or statements, criticizing the Roman Catholic Church.

The religious conflict called the Thirty Years' War was ended by the Peace of Westphalia, signed in 1648.

Through the 18th century, Germany was made up of many small states. However, in the 1700s, Prussia began to become more powerful. Prussian king Frederick II, known as Frederick the Great, added more territory to his kingdom.

In 1862, Prussian king Wilhelm I named Otto von Bismarck chancellor of Prussia, or head of the government. Bismarck's goal was to unify all of Germany under Prussian control. He achieved this goal in 1871. Wilhelm I became kaiser, or emperor, of the new German Empire.

By the early 20th century, Germany had built up a strong army and navy. It had also established **colonies** in Africa and the Asia-Pacific region. In World War I, Germany fought against France, the United Kingdom, Russia, and the United States. When Germany was defeated in 1918, Wilhelm II resigned as kaiser. Other countries took over Germany's colonies, and the German Empire came to an end.

The Age of Expansion
BY THE NUMBERS

1740–1786
Years that Frederick II served as king of Prussia.

1888
Year Wilhelm II became emperor of Germany and king of Prussia.

4 Number of German colonies in Africa at the start of World War I in 1914.

King Frederick II helped Prussia become a military power in Europe.

POPULATION

Today, more than 81 million people live in Germany. That is the highest population for any country located entirely in Europe. Most Germans live in urban areas. After Berlin, Hamburg is the next-largest city, with 1.8 million people. Munich has a slightly smaller population, with 1.4 million. Cologne has about 1 million residents.

More than 8 million **immigrants** lived in Germany as of the end of 2014. Most were Turkish. Others were from Greece, Italy, Poland, Russia, Serbia, Croatia, and Spain. In 2015, more than 1 million immigrants, many of them from Syria, entered Germany.

Many German families have few children. The country's total population is staying about the same or dropping slowly only because immigrants are coming to live in Germany. Without immigrants, the population would be declining more sharply.

75% Portion of Germany's population living in urban areas.

1st Germany's world rank among countries with a low **birthrate**.

21% Portion of people age 65 or older.

Almost 12% Percentage of the population in Germany who are immigrants.

More people live in North Rhine-Westphalia than in any other state in Germany. Düsseldorf is its largest city, after Cologne, as well as its capital.

POLITICS AND GOVERNMENT

After World War I, the government was a **republic**. In 1933, the Nazi Party, led by Adolf Hitler, established a **dictatorship** called the Third Reich. Hitler started World War II in 1939 and was responsible for the **Holocaust**.

When Germany was divided after World War II, East Germany had a **communist** government until it rejoined West Germany. In West Germany, a democratic government was set up, and that is still the form of government in Germany today. The **constitution**, called the Basic Law, was approved in 1949.

The president is the country's head of state. However, the chancellor has more power to run the government. Germany's Parliament, or legislature, has two chambers. The members of the Bundestag are elected by the people. The head of the political party with the most seats in the Bundestag usually becomes chancellor. Members of the Bundesrat are appointed by Germany's 16 state governments.

6 Million Number of Jewish people who died in the Holocaust.

69 Number of seats in the Bundesrat.

2005 Year Angela Merkel, the first woman to become chancellor of Germany, took office.

The Bundestag currently has 630 members.

CULTURAL GROUPS

A variety of cultural groups live in Germany. Most people in the country are of German descent. There are also many residents of Slavic descent.

Slavic people traditionally live in Russia, Poland, and other countries of eastern and southeastern Europe. Some Slavs came to Germany when their native lands in eastern Europe were conquered by past German kingdoms. Polish mine workers moved to Germany at the end of the 19th century. Russians came after the communist **revolution** of 1917 in Russia. In recent decades, there has been much immigration to Germany from largely Slavic countries in southeastern Europe.

The Carnival of Cultures, held in Berlin every summer, celebrates the city's different groups. The four-day event ends with a large street parade.

In eastern Germany, it is a tradition for the Slavic people called Sorbs to celebrate Easter Sunday with a horse ride.

Before World War II, Jews were the largest minority group in Germany. Some were able to flee the country in the first years after Hitler came to power. However, almost all German Jews died during the Holocaust. Only a few thousand survived.

The country's official language is German. Three major **dialects** are spoken. They are Low German in the north, Central German in the Central Uplands, and Upper German in the south. The most common immigrant language is Turkish. About 2 percent of the people speak this language. Danish is spoken in the area of northern Germany near the border with Denmark.

More than two-thirds of Germans are Catholic or Protestant. People who follow each of these religions make up 34 percent of the population. About 5 percent of Germans are Muslims, or followers of the Islamic faith. More than one-fourth of the people do not practice any organized religion.

Cultural Groups BY THE NUMBERS

4 Number of official minority languages in Germany, including Danish, Frisian, Sorbian, and Romany.

100,000 Number of Jews in Germany today.

1st Rank of German among the most widely spoken languages in the European Union.

Catholics have traveled to worship at the Pilgrimage Church of Wies in southern Germany since the mid-1700s. A pilgrimage is a journey to a holy place.

ARTS AND ENTERTAINMENT

Germany's cultural life is vibrant throughout the country. State and city governments, as well as the national government, support many theaters, museums, and concert halls. There are also private art and music institutions.

German writers are honored across the world. One of the world's most widely read books is *The Diary of a Young Girl*, written by Holocaust victim Anne Frank. It has sold more than 30 million copies. Johann Wolfgang von Goethe and Friedrich Schiller wrote poetry, novels, and plays in the 18th century. They worked in the *Sturm und Drang*, or "Storm and Stress," style, emphasizing emotion and rebellion. Modern authors Hermann Hesse, Thomas Mann, and Günter Grass have all won the Nobel Prize for Literature.

The Diary of a Young Girl by Anne Frank has been translated into more than 60 languages.

In the 19th century, the Brothers Grimm published traditional folktales, or fairy tales, with illustrations. One of the best-known stories is "Little Red Riding Hood."

Albrecht Dürer is a well-known German painter and **engraver** who worked in the late 1400s and early 1500s. His very detailed works of art often show people or religious scenes. Caspar David Friedrich and Philipp Otto Runge painted in a style called **Romanticism**.

Germany has a rich musical history. In the 1700s, Johann Sebastian Bach composed, or wrote, music in the **Baroque** style. Ludwig van Beethoven was a composer during the **Classical** period. The 19th century brought the Romantic era of music. This period featured the work of Robert Schumann and Richard Wagner. Modern composer Richard Strauss wrote symphonic poems, which are works of music inspired by a piece of writing or art.

The German movie industry flourished between 1919 and 1933. F. W. Murnau completed the silent thriller *Nosferatu* in 1922. *Metropolis*, directed by Fritz Lang, became one of the world's first science-fiction films in 1926. After World War II, a new style of realistic movies developed. Today's German directors include Wim Wenders, Werner Herzog, and Caroline Link.

Arts and Entertainment BY THE NUMBERS

MORE THAN 5,600
Total number of museums in Germany.

9 Number of symphonies Ludwig van Beethoven wrote.

1999 Year Günter Grass was awarded the Nobel Prize for Literature.

2001 Year *Nowhere in Africa*, written and directed by Caroline Link, won the Academy Award for Best Foreign Language Film.

Ludwig van Beethoven's only opera, *Fidelio*, was written in 1805. It is still performed today.

SPORTS

occer, known as football in Germany, is the country's most popular sport to play and watch. The German Football Association has more than 6 million members. In the 1970s, Franz Beckenbauer led the Bayern Munich team to three European Cup titles in a row. When he served as captain of the national team in 1974 and manager in 1990, Germany won the World Cup. Overall, the men's national team has won four World Cups, including in 2014. In 2003 and 2007, Germany won two women's World Cups in a row.

Miroslav Klose of the German national soccer team set the all-time record for World Cup goals in 2014.

The country has produced some of the world's best tennis players. In 1985, Boris Becker, at age 17, became the youngest man to win the Wimbledon men's singles championship. Wimbledon is one of the four major tennis tournaments held each year that are known as Grand Slam events. During his career, Becker won a total of six Grand Slam singles titles. In 1988, Steffi Graf won all four Grand Slam tournaments, as well as a gold medal at the Olympics. No one has ever repeated this feat, called a Golden Slam.

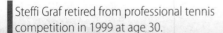

Steffi Graf retired from professional tennis competition in 1999 at age 30.

Auto racing is a major sport in Germany. The German Formula One Grand Prix is held in the summer at the Hockenheim or Nürburgring track. Michael Schumacher was Germany's top Formula One driver. He won the World Championship in 1994 and 1995. He also won every year from 2000 to 2004. His seven Formula One titles are a world record. Schumacher also holds the world record for the most Grand Prix race victories.

Germans and others ski in the Alps for fun and exercise. For those who want to compete on the snow, the annual Four Hills tournament takes place in Germany and Austria. Since this ski jumping competition began in 1952, the winner has most often been from Germany. Many people come to see it live, and millions watch on television.

Sports BY THE NUMBERS

22 Total number of Grand Slam singles titles won by Steffi Graf.

91 Number of Grand Prix races won by Michael Schumacher.

2013 Year Nadine Angerer of Germany became the first goalkeeper named the FIFA Women's World Player of the Year.

Martin Schmitt of Germany won 28 World Cup competitions in ski jumping during his career.

Mapping Germany

W e use many tools to interpret maps and to find the locations of features such as cities, states, lakes, and rivers. The map below has tools to help interpret information on the map of Germany.

Map of Germany

North Sea

Baltic Sea

• Hamburg

Oder River

★ **Berlin**

52°N

•Cologne

•Dresden

•Frankfurt

Rhine River

•Stuttgart

48°N

•Munich

Lake Constance

▲Zugspitze

8°E   12°E   16°E

MAP LEGEND

★ Capital City   ⌒ River   ╲ Longitude & Latitude
● City   -·-· Country Border   ▢ Germany
🖎 Body of Water   ▲ Mountain   ▢ Other Countries

SCALE

0 ▭▭▭ 100 Miles

0 ▭▭▭ 100 Kilometers

N
W   E
S

Mapping Tools

- The compass rose shows north, south, east, and west. The points in between represent northeast, northwest, southeast, and southwest.
- The map scale shows that the distances on a map represent much longer distances in real life. If you measure the distance between objects on a map, you can use the map scale to calculate the actual distance in miles or kilometers between those two points.
- The lines of latitude and longitude are long lines that appear on maps. The lines of latitude run east to west and measure how far north or south of the equator a place is located. The lines of longitude run north to south and measure how far east or west of the Prime Meridian a place is located. A location on a map can be found by using the two numbers where latitude and longitude meet. This number is called a coordinate and is written using degrees and direction. For example, the city of Berlin would be found at 52°N and 13°E on a map.

Map It!

Using the map and the appropriate tools, complete the activities below.

Locating with latitude and longitude
1. Which body of water is located at 48°N and 9°E?
2. Which mountain is located at 47°N and 11°E?
3. Which city is found at 48°N and 12°E?

Distances between points
4. Using the map scale and a ruler, calculate the approximate distance between Berlin and Frankfurt.
5. Using the map scale and a ruler, calculate the approximate distance between Berlin and Hamburg.
6. Using the map scale and a ruler, calculate the approximate distance between Cologne and Stuttgart.

ANSWERS 1. Lake Constance 2. Zugspitze 3. Munich 4. 265 miles (426 km) 5. 159 miles (256 km) 6. 180 miles (290 km)

Quiz Time

Test your knowledge of Germany by answering these questions.

1 What is the capital of Germany?

2 What is the name of the mountain range in the south of Germany?

3 What is the longest river in Germany?

4 What percentage of Germany is covered by forests?

5 In what city is the largest Gothic cathedral in northern Europe located?

6 What portion of the cars produced in Germany are exported?

7 In which year was the Treaty of Verdun signed?

8 Who started the Protestant Reformation?

9 What is the German constitution called?

10 How many symphonies did Ludwig van Beethoven compose?

ANSWERS
1. Berlin
2. Alps
3. Rhine
4. 32 percent
5. Cologne
6. About three-fourths
7. 843
8. Martin Luther
9. The Basic Law
10. Nine

Key Words

alpine: relating to high mountains

altitude: the height of a point in relation to sea level

Baroque: a European style in the arts that began in Italy in the 1600s and spread elsewhere into the 1700s

basins: natural depressions, or low areas, on Earth's surface, sometimes containing water

birthrate: the number of births in a year per 1,000 people in a country or area

Classical: a style of European music from 1750 to 1820

coalfields: large areas where there is much coal below the ground

colonies: countries or areas under the control of another country

communist: a system of government in which a single party controls all businesses and agriculture and all property is publicly owned

constitution: a written document stating a country's basic principles and laws

dialects: versions of a language that are spoken or known only in certain areas or by certain groups of people

dictatorship: a form of government in which leaders have complete power over their people and may govern in a cruel or unfair way

dynasty: a series of rulers from the same family

economy: the wealth and resources of a country or area

empire: a group of nations or territories headed by a single ruler

engraver: an artist who carves into a hard surface used for printing

European Union: an economic and political organization of 28 countries

exported: sold to other countries

Gothic: a style of architecture common in Europe from the 1100s to the 1500s

Holocaust: the large-scale murder of European Jews and others by the Nazis during World War II

immigrants: people who move to a new country or area to live and work

imports: goods bought from another country

plateaus: areas of flat land at high elevations, or heights above sea level

potash: a substance that contains potassium and is mostly used for fertilizers

prehistoric: referring to the period in the distant past before history was written down

republic: a form of government in which the head of state is elected

retailing: the business of selling goods to people, such as in stores, for their own use

revolution: a sudden complete change in a country's government

Roman province: a region conquered and controlled by Ancient Rome

Romanticism: a style of European art, music, and literature that lasted from the 1700s to the mid-1800s

species: groups of individuals with common characteristics

UNESCO: the United Nations Educational, Scientific, and Cultural Organization whose main goals are to promote world peace and eliminate poverty through education, science, and culture

urban: relating to a city or town

Index

Log on to www.av2books.com

AV² by Weigl brings you media enhanced books that support active learning. Go to www.av2books.com, and enter the special code found on page 2 of this book. You will gain access to enriched and enhanced content that supplements and complements this book. Content includes video, audio, weblinks, quizzes, a slide show, and activities.

AV² Online Navigation

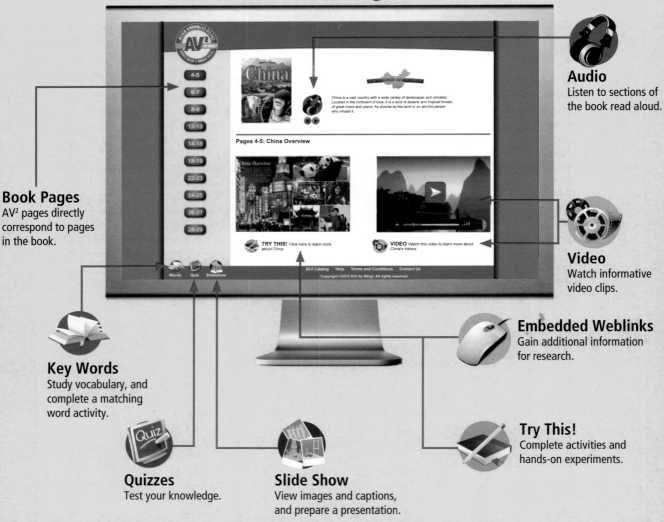

Book Pages
AV² pages directly correspond to pages in the book.

Audio
Listen to sections of the book read aloud.

Video
Watch informative video clips.

Key Words
Study vocabulary, and complete a matching word activity.

Embedded Weblinks
Gain additional information for research.

Quizzes
Test your knowledge.

Slide Show
View images and captions, and prepare a presentation.

Try This!
Complete activities and hands-on experiments.

AV² was built to bridge the gap between print and digital. We encourage you to tell us what you like and what you want to see in the future.

Sign up to be an AV² Ambassador at www.av2books.com/ambassador.

Due to the dynamic nature of the Internet, some of the URLs and activities provided as part of AV² by Weigl may have changed or ceased to exist. AV² by Weigl accepts no responsibility for any such changes. All media enhanced books are regularly monitored to update addresses and sites in a timely manner. Contact AV² by Weigl at 1-866-649-3445 or av2books@weigl.com with any questions, comments, or feedback.